Sea Turtles

By Mara Grunbaum

Children's Press®

An Imprint of Scholastic Inc.

Content Consultant
Becky Ellsworth
Curator, Shores Region
Columbus Zoo and Aquarium

Library of Congress Cataloging-in-Publication Data
Names: Grunbaum, Mara, author.
Title: Sea turtles/by Mara Grunbaum.
Other titles: Nature's children (New York, N.Y.)
Description: New York, NY: Children's Press, an imprint of Scholastic Inc.,
2018. | Series: Nature's children | Includes bibliographical references and index.
Identifiers: LCCN 2017036400| ISBN 9780531234808 (library binding) |
ISBN 9780531245101 (pbk.)
Subjects: LCSH: Sea turtles—Juvenile literature.
Classification: LCC QL666.C536 G78 2018 | DDC 597.92/8—dc23
LC record available at https://lccn.loc.gov/2017036400

Design by Anna Tunick Tabachnik

Creative Direction: Judith Christ-Lafond for Scholastic

Produced by Spooky Cheetah Press

Printed in North Mankato, MN, USA   113

SCHOLASTIC, CHILDREN'S PRESS, NATURE'S CHILDREN™, and associated logos
are trademarks and/or registered trademarks of Scholastic Inc.

1 2 3 4 5 6 7 8 9 10 R 27 26 25 24 23 22 21 20 19 18

Scholastic Inc., 557 Broadway, New York, NY 10012.

Photographs ©: cover: Monica & Michael Sweet/Getty ImagesGetty Images; 1: Rich Carey/Shutterstock; 4 leaf silo and
throughout: stockgraphicdesigns.com; 5 top turtles and throughout: Maquiladora/Shutterstock; 5 child silo: All-Silhouettes.
com; 5 bottom: Reinhard Dirscherl/ullstein bild/Getty Images; 7: Ingo Arndt/Minden Pictures; 8-9: Andrey Armyagov/
Shutterstock; 11: Pete Oxford/Minden Pictures; 13: Gerald Nowak/imageBROKER/age fotostock; 14-15: Searsie/Getty Images;
16-17: Gerard Soury/Getty Images; 18-19: Gabriel Visintin/EyeEm/Getty Images; 20: Michael Pitts/Nature Picture Library/
Getty Images; 23: USFWS Photo/Alamy Images; 24-25: Ariadne Van Zandbergen/Getty Images; 27: Stephen Frink Collection/
Alamy Images; 28-29: Visuals Unlimited, Inc./Solvin Zankl/Getty Images; 31 top left: Luis Javier Sandoval/Getty Images; 31 top
right: CK Ma/Shutterstock; 31 bottom left: Naluphoto/Dreamstime; 31 bottom right: FlavoredPixels/Shutterstock; 33: Frederic
A. Lucas/Wikimedia; 34-35: Sista Vongjintanaruks/Shutterstock; 37: Jeff Rotman/Getty Images; 38-39: piluhin/Alamy Images;
40-41: PABLO COZZAGLIO/AFP/Getty Images; 42 bottom left: Pete Oxford/Minden Pictures; 42 bottom right: Nick Henn/
Shutterstock; 42 top left: AppStock/Shutterstock; 42 top right: Anankkml/Dreamstime; 43 bottom left: George Grail/Getty
Images; 43 top left: Smileus/Dreamstime; 43 top right: Smit/Shutterstock; 43 bottom right: Rich Carey/Shutterstock.

Maps by Jim McMahon.

Table of Contents

Fact File: Sea Turtles

World Distribution
Oceans around the world
and the Mediterranean Sea

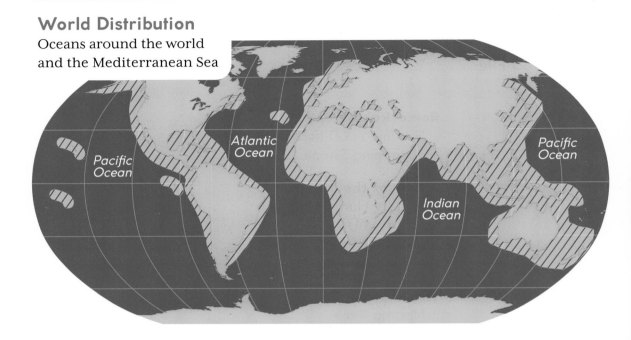

Population Status
Two species
critically
endangered; one
endangered; three
vulnerable; one
unknown

Habitats
Tropical oceans,
coastal waters, and
shallow beaches

Habits
Live mostly
underwater but
surface to breathe;
lay eggs on beaches;
can migrate
hundreds or even
thousands of miles
for food and egg
laying

Diet
Most sea turtles
feed on ocean life
such as jellyfish,
sponges, urchins,
fish, and crabs;
green sea turtles
eat seagrasses

Distinctive Features
Protective shell
that is smooth
and leathery on
leatherback sea
turtles and hard
and bony on others;
four paddle-like
flippers; hard, spiky
jaw and no teeth

Fast Fact
Sea turtles nest
on every continent
except Antarctica.

Average Size

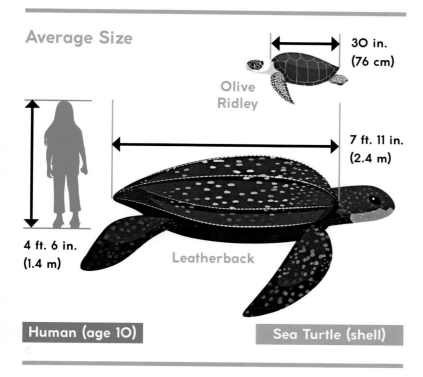

Olive Ridley

30 in.
(76 cm)

7 ft. 11 in.
(2.4 m)

4 ft. 6 in.
(1.4 m)

Leatherback

Human (age 10)

Sea Turtle (shell)

Taxonomy

CLASS
Reptilia (reptiles)

ORDER
Testudines (turtles, tortoises, terrapins)

FAMILY
Cheloniidae (hard-shelled sea turtles) and Dermochelyidae (leatherback sea turtles)

GENERA
6 genera

SPECIES
- *Caretta caretta* (loggerhead)
- *Chelonia mydas* (green)
- *Eretmochelys imbricata* (hawksbill)
- *Lepidochelys kempii* (Kemp's ridley)
- *Lepidochelys olivacea* (olive ridley)
- *Natator depressus* (flatback)
- *Dermochelys coriacea* (leatherback)

CHAPTER 1

Remarkable Reptiles

It's almost midnight in Costa Rica, Central America. The swimmers and sunbathers have all left the beach. Under the bright moonlight, waves break against the shore.

Suddenly a spot on the beach starts twitching. A tiny flipper pokes out of the sand. It's followed by another flipper, then a head, and then a shell. A nest of baby sea turtles is hatching. Hundreds of them will try to reach the water tonight.

Sea turtles are reptiles. As babies, they're no bigger than golf balls. But some grow up to be 8 feet (2.5 meters) long and weigh nearly 2,000 pounds (907.2 kilograms).

There are seven species of sea turtle. Several of those are endangered. That means they could die out unless their circumstances change.

▶ Olive ridley hatchlings hurry to the sea near this Costa Rican beach.

Fast Fact
Sea turtles are among the largest reptiles on Earth.

Similar, Yet Different

All seven species of sea turtle share common traits—from how their bodies are built to the habitats they favor. But each one is also unique in many ways. Most sea turtles are spread far across the world. However, the flatback sea turtle lives only in Australia and Papua New Guinea.

Although sea turtles' bodies look very similar, each species has distinctive features. The loggerhead sea turtle is named for its large skull. The hawksbill sea turtle has a face that comes to a sharp point, like a bird's beak.

The smallest sea turtle is the Kemp's ridley. It weighs only about 100 lb. (45.4 kg). The leatherback sea turtle can be 20 times as heavy. It's the largest living turtle in the world.

◀ Hawksbill sea turtles use their beaklike mouths to eat ocean sponges.

9

Swimming Shape

Like a fish or a dolphin, a sea turtle is built for life at sea. Its strong, sleek body moves quickly through the water. This body shape is an **adaptation** that helps the sea turtle survive.

Sea turtles have four limbs that they use for swimming. They paddle with their strong front flippers. Their nimble back flippers help them steer. On land, they use all four flippers to drag themselves across the sand.

All species except the leatherback have a bony outer shell. This tough covering protects sea turtles from **predators**. But unlike many other turtles, sea turtles can't pull their heads or limbs inside.

Sea turtles have no teeth. Instead, they use their powerful jaws to crush food. The green sea turtle's jaw even has knifelike ridges. Sea turtles' mouths and throats are lined with hard spikes. Soft **prey**, such as jellyfish, get snagged on the spikes. Once they do, there's no escape.

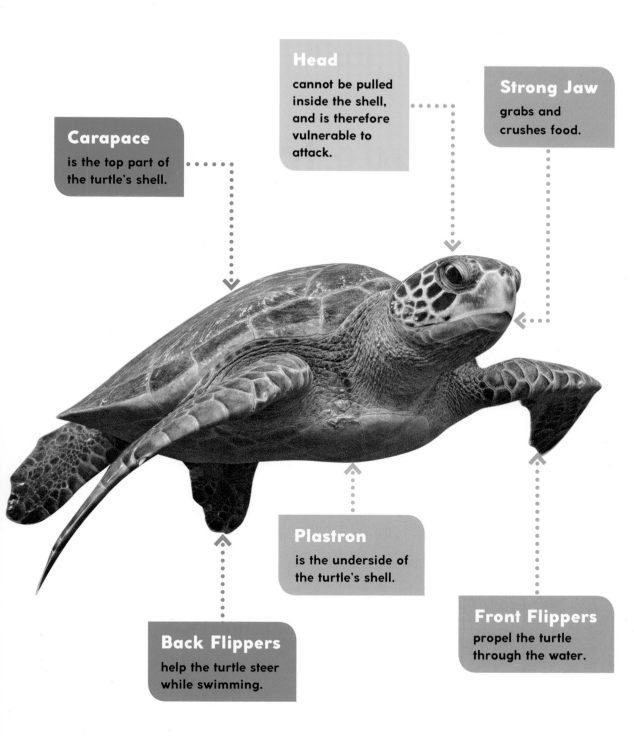

Carapace
is the top part of
the turtle's shell.

Head
cannot be pulled
inside the shell,
and is therefore
vulnerable to
attack.

Strong Jaw
grabs and
crushes food.

Plastron
is the underside of
the turtle's shell.

Back Flippers
help the turtle steer
while swimming.

Front Flippers
propel the turtle
through the water.

CHAPTER 2

Made for the Water

If a sea turtle raced an Olympic swimmer, the turtle would win every time. The fastest human swimmer can travel 6 miles per hour (9.7 kilometers per hour) underwater. A sea turtle's top speed is 22 mph (35.5 kph). That's three times as fast!

Being strong swimmers is important. Green sea turtles occasionally bask on beaches. But other species come onshore only to lay eggs. They could be at sea for decades before then.

Like other reptiles, sea turtles are cold-blooded. Their body temperature depends on the air or water around them. That's why most sea turtles stay in the warm waters of the tropics. But the leatherback has an advantage. Its massive body loses heat more slowly. That means it can swim in the colder waters of Alaska and beyond.

▶ A green sea turtle can hold its breath for a long time as it dives for food.

Hungry Hunters

Sea turtles need lots of energy to keep swimming. They spend the majority of their day looking for food.

Green sea turtles are strictly **herbivores**. They eat **algae**, seagrasses, and seaweed. Other sea turtles are **carnivores**. Each species has a different favorite food. Hawksbill sea turtles eat mostly sponges. The Kemp's ridley sea turtle prefers crabs. The leatherback's jaw isn't strong enough to crush animals with shells. It sticks to soft prey such as jellyfish. Leatherbacks also eat squishy animals called salps.

A single jellyfish isn't very filling. Enormous leatherbacks eat as many as they can find. But this appetite can be a problem in a polluted ocean. Many sea turtles mistake floating trash for food. Leatherbacks often swallow plastic bags they think are jellyfish. But the turtles can't digest these materials. If they eat the plastic bags, they can become very sick or die.

◄ Loggerhead sea turtles eat jellyfish, crabs, snails, and other boneless animals.

Armored Up

A sea turtle's shell is part of its skeleton. It's made up of more than 50 bones. On most species, both the carapace and plastron are covered with scaly plates called scutes. The plates are made of the same hard material as human fingernails. They add an extra layer of protection to the shell below.

Each sea turtle species has a different number and pattern of scutes. Green sea turtles have a starburst shape on each plate. Leatherback sea turtles have no scutes at all. They're covered with dark, leathery skin instead.

Thanks to these built-in shields, adult sea turtles have few natural predators. However, sharks, orcas, and crocodiles are all strong enough to crush a turtle's armor. People have also killed sea turtles to make jewelry from their shells.

▶ The green sea turtle's shell has a distinctive pattern on each scute.

Deep Breaths

Even though sea turtles live underwater, they need to breathe air. Most swim to the surface every few minutes when they're awake. But they can stay underwater longer to rest and feed.

Olive ridley sea turtles dive about 500 ft. (152.4 m) below the surface to eat snails and crabs on the seafloor. But leatherbacks are the champion divers. They can swim 4,200 ft. (1,280.2 m) deep in search of food. It's worth it if they find a school of jellyfish. A leatherback can feed for almost an hour and a half without coming up for air.

Resting turtles use less energy, so they can breathe less often. A sleeping sea turtle may stay underwater for four to seven hours. It wedges itself beneath a rock so that it won't drift away. In the open ocean, turtles sleep at the water's surface with their nostrils poking out of the water. They bob along with the current until they're ready to wake up and swim.

◀ A green sea turtle lifts its head above the surface of the water to breathe.

Navigation All-Stars

Even with advanced navigation tools, people can get lost at sea. That doesn't happen to sea turtles. That's because the reptiles have a rare ability. They navigate by sensing Earth's magnetic field.

The magnetic field is an invisible force that surrounds the planet. It's what makes compasses point north. Humans can't detect this force without assistance. But sea turtles can feel it with their bodies. It helps them figure out where they are and which way to go.

This special sense helps sea turtles travel extremely long distances. Green sea turtles, for instance, migrate up to 2,800 mi. (4,506.2 km). But leatherback sea turtles hold the record. Some of them swim all the way across the Pacific Ocean. That's a distance of almost 7,000 mi. (11,265.4 km). It can take them up to a year. But with the magnetic field to guide them, they know exactly where to go.

▶ There are no landmarks for this sea turtle to follow as it navigates through the open ocean.

CHAPTER 3

The Life of a Sea Turtle

Sea turtles can migrate over huge distances to find food, move to warmer waters, and lay eggs. That makes it hard for scientists to follow them and find out how long they live. It is even difficult to tell how old a sea turtle in **captivity** may be. Experts do know they live very long lives, though. Some species don't even **reproduce** until they're 50 years old!

During those years a sea turtle goes through many changes. It also covers thousands of miles at sea. But at nesting time, there's only one place all sea turtles want to go: to the beach. Many species return to the exact same beaches where they were born. They lay their eggs in the sand that they came from.

▶ Green sea turtles come ashore to lay eggs on Midway Island in the Pacific Ocean.

Nesting Time

Every two or three years, sea turtles come together to mate. This takes place at sea. Then the female climbs onto land. She crawls above the high-tide line and digs a hole with her flippers. She lays her eggs inside. Then she takes her time to bury her eggs carefully. She uses her flippers to cover the nest with sand to hide it from predators and keep the eggs warm. Then she returns to the sea.

For many species, the female makes her journey to the beach alone. Kemp's ridley and olive ridley sea turtles do things a little differently. They nest in groups. Every year, thousands of ridley sea turtles come ashore at the same time to nest. This amazing event is called an *arribada*—a Spanish word that means "arrival." Female turtles cover the entire beach.

Each sea turtle egg is about the size of a golf ball. A female can lay more than 100 in one nest. She repeats this process five or more times during a nesting season. Some species may lay more than 1,000 eggs in a season!

◄ A leatherback sea turtle lays her eggs on a beach in South America.

25

Breakout!

Sea turtle eggs **incubate** underground for 40 to 70 days. How they develop depends on the temperature of the nest. If the sand is cool, most eggs become male turtles. If it's warmer, they'll be females. At just the right temperature, there will be an even mix. This happens around 85°F (29°C).

When the baby turtles are ready, they hatch. Most of the babies in a nest hatch at the same time. At this point they weigh less than 1.5 ounces (42.5 grams) apiece. Each one has a sharp, toothlike point on its upper jaw. It uses this to tear open the leathery egg.

The next task is to dig to the sand's surface. A single hatchling isn't strong enough to do this on its own. Once most of the babies have hatched, they stand on top of their empty eggshells. They scratch at the top and sides of the nest with their little front flippers. This process can take the hatchlings several days. By working together, they eventually break through.

▶ Loggerhead hatchlings emerge from their shells and scramble out of their nest.

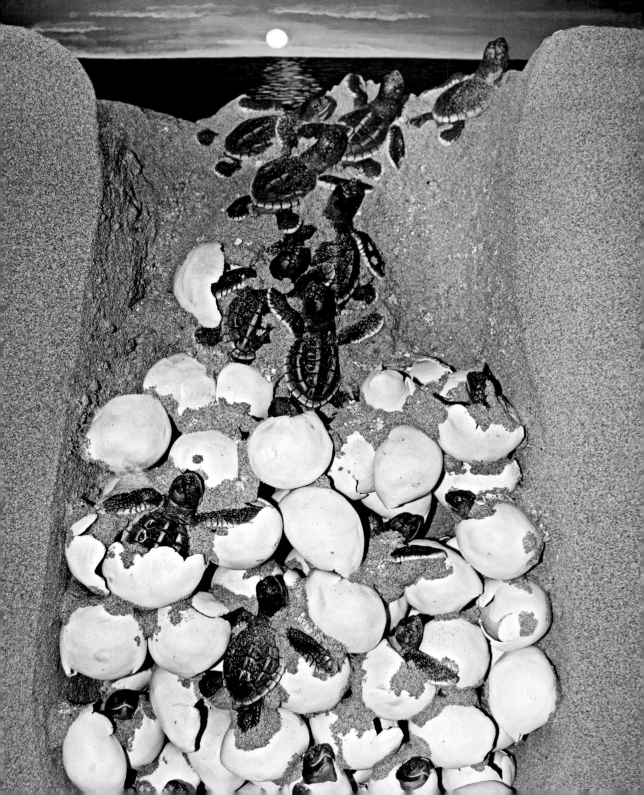

Race to the Ocean

Escaping the sand isn't the only hard part of hatching. Once the newborn sea turtles have emerged, they must immediately scurry to the sea.

Sea turtles are born with the **instinct** to move toward the water. They use their tiny flippers to crawl across the sand. Most baby sea turtles emerge at night. They can see the bright moonlight reflecting off the water. It tells them which way to go.

But the hatchlings' journey is very dangerous. Seabirds, crabs, and other predators roam the beach, too. They can easily snatch the baby turtles off the sand. Many of the babies get eaten. Only the luckiest ones make it to the ocean. When they do, they throw themselves into the waves.

The water isn't always safe, either. Young sea turtles are small and can be swallowed by swimming predators such as dolphinfish. Fewer than one in 1,000 sea turtle hatchlings survive to become adults.

◀ A wood stork snags a baby sea turtle on its way to the ocean in Costa Rica.

Reef Rescuers

Once a hatchling reaches the water, it won't touch land again for many years. Juvenile sea turtles stay in the open ocean. They live in masses of sargassum, a weedy floating plant. Many invertebrates also live in the sargassum. The sea turtles can feed and hide from predators in the weeds. Some sea turtles remain in the open ocean for decades. But as adults, they move closer to shore. There, they meet and reproduce with other turtles. They find food and shelter around coral reefs. These habitats are also home to millions of other species.

Green sea turtles are an especially important part of the coral reef ecosystem. They graze on algae and grasses that grow on the reef. These plants would smother the corals if turtles didn't eat them. By cleaning the corals, sea turtles help keep all the reef species alive.

▶ These are just a few of the species sea turtles interact with at a reef.

Brain Coral

Sea turtles help keep corals, like this one, clean.

Coral Crab

Sea turtles may prey on crabs that feed on reefs.

Tiger Shark

▶ These predators hunt reef animals. The largest can eat adult sea turtles.

Yellow Tang

▶ These reef fish help keep turtles healthy by eating pests that grow on their shells.

Ancient Creatures

About 220 million years ago, Earth looked very different from how it does today. There were no mammals, birds, lizards, or flowering plants. Dinosaurs were just beginning to roam the land. It was in this ancient landscape that the first turtles appeared.

Early turtles lived in soggy marshland. They **evolved** and spread into new habitats over time. Some turtles moved onto dry land. They made their homes in forests, grasslands, and even deserts. Other turtles became water dwellers. They swam into lakes and rivers around the world. Around 110 million years ago, a group of turtles started living in the ocean. They were the **ancestors** of sea turtles that live today.

The largest turtle ever known is called *Stupendemys*. It lived in freshwater about 5 million years ago. Scientists have found **fossils** of this giant turtle in Venezuela and Brazil, South America. Its shell was up to 7.5 ft. (2.3 m) long.

▶ *Archelon*, an extinct sea turtle, was about 11 ft. (3.4 m) from snout to tail.

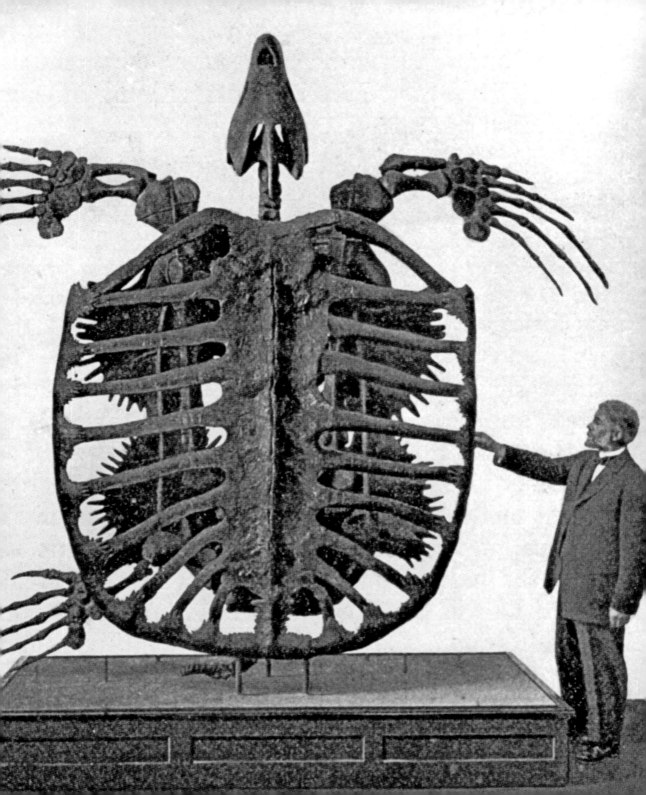

A Tough Family

Dinosaurs may seem like the toughest ancient animals. But they became **extinct** 65 million years ago. And turtles are still here! Today, there are more than 300 species of turtles. They live in almost every habitat on Earth.

The largest, the leatherback, makes its home in the sea. One of the smallest, the speckled Cape tortoise, can be found on land. It is only 3.5 in. (8.9 cm) long. All turtles have some characteristics in common. They have no teeth and lay their eggs in nests. And all but a few species have a hard, bony shell.

Sea turtles can't pull their heads, tails, or legs into their shells. But other turtle species can. They withdraw into their shells when they feel threatened. Some species, such as box turtles, can even snap their shells all the way closed.

About half of all turtle species are endangered. Many could become extinct within decades—if not sooner.

◀ Alligator snapping turtles are freshwater turtles that have strong jaws and distinctive spiky shells.

CHAPTER 5

Critical Condition

Sea turtles face many threats.

Unfortunately, most of them come from humans. In some parts of the world, people eat the turtles and their eggs. Hawksbill shells are used to make jewelry. People turn their skin into leather. Sea turtles also get hit by boats or become tangled in fishing nets.

Climate change is an even bigger problem. Warming water threatens the coral reefs where sea turtles live. Climate change is bad for sea turtle nests, too. If the sand gets too hot, most hatchlings will be female. Without enough males, the turtles can't reproduce.

Hawksbill and Kemp's ridley sea turtles are critically endangered. There's an extremely high risk that they will die out in the wild. Green sea turtles are also endangered. Other species are doing better, but their numbers are still falling. Over the past several decades, the population of leatherbacks has dropped by about 40 percent.

▶ Every year, thousands of turtles get caught in fishing nets and drown.

Trouble at the Beach

Sea turtles nest on beaches around the world. But people use many of those areas, too. They visit the beach and build homes and stores along the shore. This can cause problems for sea turtles and their young.

Baby sea turtles use moonlight to guide them to the water. But bright lights from buildings can confuse them. They may crawl toward the buildings instead of the ocean—and most likely die. People and dogs may also disturb mother turtles or their nests on the beach.

Officials and beachgoers can work together to solve these problems. Authorities may mark turtle nesting spots to warn people to leave them alone. The beach in Mexico where Kemp's ridley sea turtles nest is a national reserve. In Florida, many beachfront buildings have replaced their lightbulbs. They shade the lights to make them less visible from the sand. The darker the beach, the better the odds that the turtles will survive.

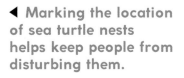

◀ Marking the location of sea turtle nests helps keep people from disturbing them.

A Helping Hand

There's a special hospital in Marathon, Florida. Its patients are sick and injured sea turtles. Some of them have swallowed plastic. Others have been wounded in boat accidents. Most would die without people's help.

The Turtle Hospital staff picks up sick sea turtles in the area. Veterinarians treat the turtles and help their injuries heal. It can take many months for each turtle to recover. If a turtle was very badly injured, it may have to stay under human care. But many patients can be released back into the wild. The hospital has released more than 1,500 sea turtles since 1986.

People around the world can help sea turtles, too. Using less plastic is one good step. The cleaner we can keep the oceans, the better sea turtles will do.

Sea turtles are tough creatures. They're built to survive a lot of natural threats. But the world is changing quickly around them. After many millions of years on Earth, the time has finally come where they need our help to survive.

▶ Veterinarians at The Turtle Hospital operate on an injured Kemp's ridley sea turtle.

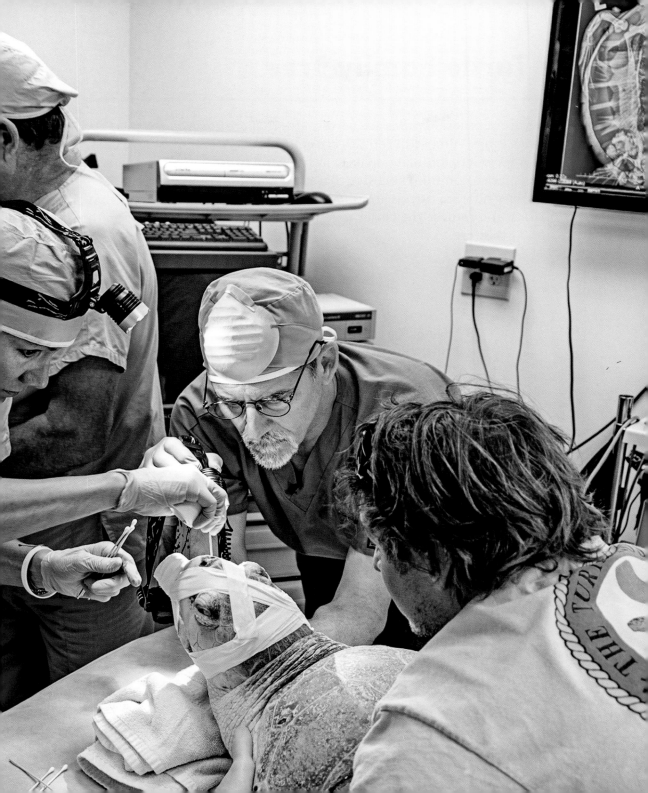

Sea Turtle Family Tree

Sea turtles are reptiles. Reptiles are vertebrates that are covered in scales and breathe with lungs. Almost all reptiles are cold-blooded, and most lay eggs. Reptiles comprise crocodilians, snakes, lizards, and turtles, among others. All reptiles share a common ancestor that lived 300 million years ago. This diagram shows how sea turtles are related to other reptiles and animals that are descended from reptiles. The closer together two animals are on the tree, the more similar they are.

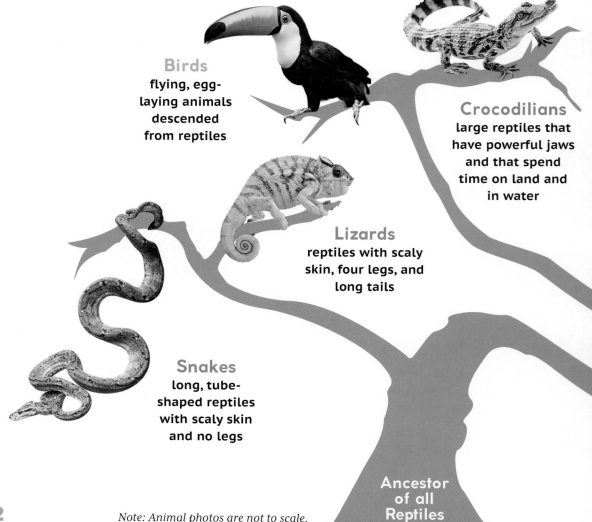

Birds
flying, egg-laying animals descended from reptiles

Crocodilians
large reptiles that have powerful jaws and that spend time on land and in water

Lizards
reptiles with scaly skin, four legs, and long tails

Snakes
long, tube-shaped reptiles with scaly skin and no legs

Ancestor of all Reptiles

Note: Animal photos are not to scale.

Tortoises
large, land-dwelling turtles with domed shells

Pond Turtles
small freshwater turtles that can retract into their shells

Softshell Turtles
flat turtles with long snouts and leathery shells

Sea Turtles
ocean-dwelling turtles with strong front flippers

Words to Know

A........ **adaptation** *(ad-ap-TAY-shun)* change a living thing goes through so it fits in better within its environment

algae *(AL-jee)* small plants without roots or stems that grow mainly in water

ancestors *(ANN-sess-turs)* family members who lived long ago

C........ **captivity** *(kap-TIV-i-tee)* the condition of living in the care of people

carapace *(KARE-uh-pis)* the bony shell on the back of a turtle or other animal

carnivores *(KAHR-nuh-vorz)* animals that eat meat

climate change *(KLYE-mat chaynj)* global warming and other changes in weather and weather patterns that are happening because of human activity

E........ **ecosystem** *(EE-koh-sis-tuhm)* all the living things in a place and their relation to their environment

endangered *(en-DAYN-juhrd)* a plant or animal that is in danger of becoming extinct, usually because of human activity

evolved *(i-VAHLVD)* changed slowly and naturally over time

extinct *(ik-STINGKT)* no longer found alive

F........ **fossils** *(FAH-suhls)* bones, shells, or other traces of an animal or plant from millions of years ago, preserved as rock

H........ **herbivores** *(HUR-buh-vorz)* animals that eat only plants

I .... **incubate** *(ING-kyuh-bayt)* to keep eggs warm before they hatch

instinct *(IN-stingkt)* behavior that is natural rather than learned

invertebrates *(in-VUHR-tuh-brits)* animals without a backbone

J .... **juvenile** *(JOO-vuh-nyle)* in the life stage between infancy and adulthood

M .... **migrate** *(MYE-grate)* to move to another area or climate at a particular time of year

P .... **plastron** *(PLASS-trohn)* the bony shell on the underside of a turtle

predators *(PRED-uh-tuhrs)* animals that live by hunting other animals for food

prey *(PRAY)* an animal that is hunted by another animal for food

R .... **reproduce** *(ree-pruh-DOOS)* to produce offspring or individuals of the same kind

reptiles *(REP-tilez)* cold-blooded animals that crawl across the ground or creep on short legs; most have backbones and reproduce by laying eggs

reserve *(rih-ZERV)* protected place where hunting is not allowed and where animals can live and breed safely

S .... **scutes** *(SCOOTS)* flexible pieces of fingernail-like material that form a turtle's shell

species *(SPEE-sheez)* one of the groups into which animals and plants are divided; members of the same species can mate and have offspring

T .... **tropics** *(TRAH-piks)* the extremely hot area of Earth near the equator

Find Out More

BOOKS

- Riggs, Kate. *Sea Turtles*. Mankato, MN: The Creative Company, 2016.
- Swinburne, Stephen R. *Sea Turtle Scientist*. New York: Houghton Mifflin Harcourt, 2014.
- Young, Karen Romano. *Sea Turtle Rescue: All About Sea Turtles and How to Save Them*. Washington, D.C.: National Geographic Society, 2015.

WEB PAGES

- www.hawksbill.org

  The Web site of the Eastern Pacific Hawksbill Initiative provides a fact sheet on hawksbills, videos, a photo gallery, and information on the turtles' nests and foraging sites.

- www.seaturtlestatus.org

  Educational materials on sea turtle species, life cycle, threats, and more from the State of the World's Sea Turtles.

- www.pbs.org/wnet/nature/voyage-of-the-lonely-turtle-sea-turtle-navigation/2507

  Information from the PBS *Nature* episode "Voyage of the Lonely Sea Turtle."

Facts for Now

Visit this Scholastic Web site for more information on sea turtles:
www.factsfornow.scholastic.com Enter the keywords Sea Turtles

Index

Index *(continued)*

About the Author

Mara Grunbaum is a science writer and the editor of Scholastic's *SuperScience* magazine. She's fascinated by all animals, from wild sea turtles to her domestic cat, Zadie. She lives in Brooklyn, New York.